R AMAZING!™

We find the amazing in the ordinary everyday with lists, polls and quizzes. Helping us to appreciate, in fun and quirky ways, the world in which we live.

Creating interactive content, R Amazing! is a safe place to explore different topics and share your views.

It is ok to disagree with us regarding who or what we think is amazing! We share our thoughts on our website and in our books to enable debate and discussion.

We encourage the expression of opinions in an appropriate way with an understanding that it is ok for people to have differing views.

R Amazing! debates should be conducted politely and respectfully, ending with an agreement and common ground, even if that is to agree to disagree.

www.r-amazing.com

Pigs R Amazing!
Mark 'Markus' Baker & Adam Galvin

Published by R-and-Q.com.
Copyright © 2020 R-and-Q.com

PIGS

R AMAZING! ™

www.r-amazing.com/pigs/

Adam Galvin and Markus Baker
Creators of R Amazing!

"*Dogs look up to man.
Cats look down to man.
Pigs look us straight in the
eye and see an equal.*"

Winston Churchill

"

I've always loved
pigs: the shape
of them, the...

...look of them, and the fact that they are so intelligent.

Maurice Sendak

"

A Wheelie Good Pig

A piglet called Chris who, at birth, was discovered to not have the use of his rear legs was taken to the vets to be put down. Luckily for Chris, that vet was Dr. Len Lucero, an extremely kind and creative person, who took the little pig home to care for him.

In a stroke of imaginative genius, Dr. Lucero designed and built Chris a wheelchair-like device from his children's K'Nex building blocks.

Humorously, giving the piglet the full name of Chris P. Bacon, The vet uploaded a video of the happy looking piglet moving around with his new set of wheels. This video has more than 2.5 million views on YouTube. Dr. Lucero and Chris P. Bacon later featured in a PBS documentary titled "My Bionic Pet".

As Chris grew, his set of wheels got bigger and bigger eventually moving into a wheelchair that was designed and built for dogs.

What do you think of Dr. Lucero's creative work and the full name he gave to the pig?

A Pig's Nose

Well known for their distinctive snouts, pigs have an extremely good sense of smell. It is around 2000 times more sensitive than that of a human.

The large, round, flattened tip of a pig's nose is cartilage that is linked to muscle. This gives its snout the strength to find its food by digging around in the mud and undergrowth. Using it a little like a shovel to dig up vegetables and truffles from the ground.

If you look after pigs, remember to scatter food so they can find it with their amazing sense of smell. This helps to keep their body and minds active.

Smell is a potent wizard that transports you across thousands of miles and all the years you have lived.

Helen Keller

DID YOU KNOW?

Pigs are omnivores, meaning they eat both plants and other animals, just like humans do.

Source: http://www.sciencekids.co.nz/sciencefacts/animals/pig.html

I learned long ago, never to wrestle with a pig. You get dirty, and besides, the pig likes it.

George Bernard Shaw

Pigs and Humans

A pig's genetic makeup is very similar to our own. Scientists are now using stem cells from pigs to research cures for human diseases.

Pioneering UK surgeon, Sir Terence English believes that xenotransplantation, which is transplanting an organ from one species to another, will soon be possible. This type of surgery is most likely to be between a pig and a human.

The hope is to, at first, perform a kidney xenotransplant before working towards transplanting a pig's heart into a human being.

What are your views on xenotransplants?

The creatures outside looked from pig to man, and from man to pig, and from pig to man again; but already it was impossible to say which was which.
George Orwell

Heroic Pigs

There are several examples of pigs saving people's lives.

A pet pig called Pru pulled her owner out of a muddy bog.

Priscilla, proving that pigs can swim, saved a child who was in distress and difficulty in water.

A Mother and Daughter had a 'Lucky' escape from a fire in their home when their pig, named Lucky, alerted them to the danger.

A Vietnamese pot-bellied pig called LuLu raised the alarm to passers-by that her owner was having a heart attack.

Then there is Ludwig who protected its owner's home by chasing a gang of burglars away.

> *The greatest ethical test that we're ever going to face is the treatment of those who are at our mercy.*
> Lyn White

"

*A pig with two owners is
sure to die of hunger.*

Proverb

DID YOU KNOW?

A pig's squeal can be as loud as 115 decibels – that's 3 decibels higher than the sound of a supersonic plane.

Pigs May Fly

In 2014, on a US Airway's flight from Connecticut to Washington DC, a lady was seen carrying what many thought to be a duffel bag. It turned out to be a 70-pound pot-bellied pig that she was carrying over her shoulder.

Having been labelled an Emotional Support Animal, the pig, which was on a lead, had passed through airport security and was authorised to fly by the airline.

Unfortunately, due to the animal's poor behaviour and stinking out the aircraft, the pig and its owner were asked to leave the plane before take-off. Some reports said that the pig had pooed on the floor!

One pig, named Hamlet, had much better manners when on a plane. He even has his own Instagram channel that shares many of his adventures.

So the answer to the question 'Can pig's fly?' is yes, as long as they are well behaved.

The Pig Who Loved People

Bette had an anxiety disorder, in which she feared and avoided open spaces, known as agoraphobia. Even going to the shop could cause Bette to have a panic attack.

A friend offered Bette and her husband, Don, a pig called Lord Bacon. Stating that the pig loved people and would be nice for Bette to have around the home. Having felt helpless about Bette's condition, Don thought having a new pet was a great idea. Bette was not so sure, though after remembering that caring for an animal helps improve a person's well being, she changed her mind.

Right from the first time Bette and Lord Bacon met there was a connection that just grew and grew. All the family loved Lord Bacon and chose to rename him Pigger. This special relationship connected the family and helped Bette become more confident about going outside.

Between pigs and human beings there was not and there need not be any clash of interest whatsoever.
George Orwell

DID YOU KNOW?

Pigs were domesticated approximately 5,000 to 7,000 years ago, which is even before cows were.
Today there are around 2 billion pigs in the world.

You can't root with the hogs and have a clean nose.

Mieder

"

The Tamworth Two

On 8th January 1998, two pigs escaped whilst being unloaded from a lorry at an abattoir in Malmesbury, Wiltshire.

These two little pig's escape was widely covered in the media. They named the Tamworth boar Sundance and his sister Butch. Collectively, they were affectionately known as The Tamworth Two.

For more than a week, Butch and Sundance's escapades were shared around the world. Butch was caught first on the 15th January, followed by Sundance the next day. The original plan was to take the Tamworth Two back to the abattoir. The public's love for the 2 pigs changed this. Many different groups offered to pay for the pigs to spend the rest of their lives happily in an animal sanctuary.

This is what happened. Both pigs continued to be celebrities, with many people visiting them at The Rare Breeds Centre, an animal sanctuary in Ashford, Kent. Butch passed away in October 2010 followed by Sundance in May 2011.

In 2004, their adventures were even turned into a BBC movie titled "The Legend of The Tamworth Two".

LEARN MORE AT

www.r-amazing.com/running-pig/

A Running Pig

Are pigs fast or slow runners? You may be surprised by the answer.

Pigs are sprinters, which means they can run fast over short distances.

It is believed that a domestic pig can run at speeds of around 17 kmh (10.5 mph). Amazingly, wild pigs can run much faster, at speeds of up to 48 kmh (30 mph).

If you can run the 100 meters in less than 20 seconds, which is roughly 17.5 kmh (11 mph), you can run faster than a domestic pig. That does not necessarily mean you will catch it though because pigs generally do not run in a straight line. They prefer to zig-zag.

> *You can't make a race horse of a pig.*
> *No, said Samuel, but you*
> *can make a very fast pig.*
> John Steinbeck, East of Eden

"

Never try to teach a pig to sing. You waste your time and you annoy the pig.

Robert A. Heinlein

DID YOU KNOW?

A Gilt is a young adult female pig that has not given birth to a litter of piglets, known as farrowing.
A Sow is an adult female pig who has have farrowed one or more litters.
A Boar is an adult male pig used for mating.

LEARN MORE AT

www.r-amazing.com/hygiene-pig/

Clean Pigs

Pigs sometimes have the reputation of being dirty and messy animals, however, this is not true. They tend to roll in mud only to stay cool because they are unable to sweat.

An interesting experiment at a Zoo in Switzerland gave Boars apple slices that were covered in sand. Prior to eating, they rinsed the piece of fruit in a creek that ran through their enclosure.

The boars only washed their snack when it was dirty, if the apple was clean they would eat it straight away without washing it first.

Nine-tenths of our sickness can be prevented by right thinking plus right hygiene - nine-tenths of it!

Henry Miller

Who's a Clever Hog?

Pigs are said to be the world's fifth-most intelligent animal. They outperform 3-year-old human children on cognition tests and are believed to be even cleverer than dogs.

In 2016, Amy, a pet pig owned by Lori Stock joined a Seattle dog agility class, where she was soon labelled 'top dog'. Amy would jump through hoops, balance along the see-saw, retrieve the dumbbell and zip through a play tunnel. Lori states that Amy is a quick learner and is already outperforming the dogs. Lori goes on to share that Amy's main motivation is food. She will do almost any agility for an edible treat.

A further example of pigs outperforming dogs, and even chimpanzees, is an experiment with animals playing a video game. Each animal is required to roll a ball into a shaded area positioned on a monitor. Achieving this task would result in a food reward. With each increasing level, the shaded area reduced in size and the amount of edible reward increased. Pigs attained the highest game level in comparison to dogs and chimps.

DID YOU KNOW?

Pigs only say "Oink!" in English-speaking countries. In French, they say "Groin!" and in Polish, they say "Chrum!". This is because of onomatopoeia which is a word that phonetically resembles the sound that describes it.

Source: http://idspigs.co.uk/2016/03/10-facts-about-pigs/

Well-being and happiness never appeared to me as an absolute aim. I am even inclined to compare such moral aims to the ambitions of a pig.

Albert Einstein

"

The Wonder Pig

Believing she was a micro pig, Steve Jenkins and Derek Walter adopted Esther into their home.

Weighing just 1.4 kg (3 lb), everything started fantastically because Esther would grow to be no bigger than 32 kg (70 lb). However, Esther was not a micro pig. Esther kept growing and growing!

Steve and Derek couldn't imagine life without amazing Esther. Having decided to keep their wonderful pig, both were surprised to see her grow to be as big as 304 kg (670 lb)!

Having improved their lives due to her intelligence and kindness, Steve and Derek affectionately renamed her 'Esther the Wonder Pig'. This led both Steve and Derek to choose to follow a vegan diet. Would anything encourage you to stop eating meat to become a vegetarian or vegan?

> *It was hard on us. At our lowest point, I'd be in tears thinking we had to get rid of her.*
> Steve Jenkins

Like children, pigs thrive on affection, enjoy toys, have a short attention span, and are easily bored.

Karl Schwenke

DID YOU KNOW?

By the age of 2 weeks old, Piglets run to their mothers' voices, and can recognise their name.

My picture of the most amazing pig in the world!

The most amazing pig in the world is

I love it when this amazing pig...

....

....

....

....

....

....

This pig is amazing because...

....

....

....

....

MORE BOOKS BY R&Q

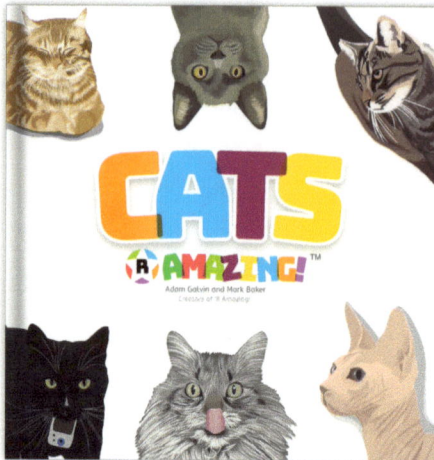

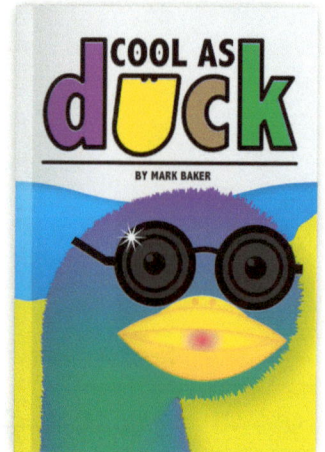

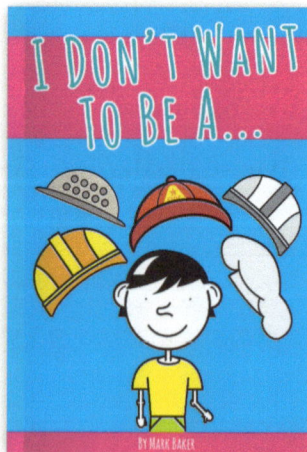

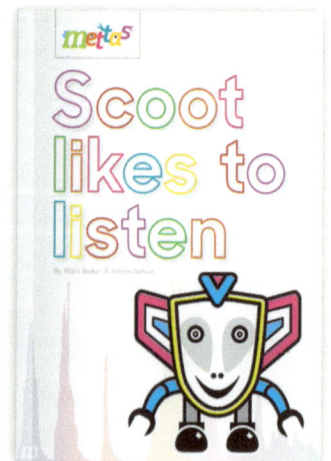

www.ingramcontent.com/pod-product-compliance
Lightning Source LLC
Chambersburg PA
CBHW060832270326
41933CB00002B/57